Animals as Friends

Sally Morgan

W
FRANKLIN WATTS
LONDON • SYDNEY

This edition 2003

Franklin Watts
96 Leonard Street
London
EC2A 4XD

Franklin Watts Australia
45-51 Huntley Street
Alexandria
NSW 2015

Copyright © Franklin Watts 1999

ISBN 0 7496 5014 1

Series editor: Helen Lanz
Series designer: Louise Snowdon
Picture research: Sue Mennell

Printed in Malaysia

Contents

Animals as friends.............................4

Good company.................................6

Planning ahead...............................8

Training your pet...........................10

A healthy life..............................12

Learning to relax...........................14

Feeling proud...............................16

A sixth sense?..............................18

Pets for protection.........................20

Saving lives................................22

The way home................................24

Saying goodbye..............................26

Old friends.................................28

Glossary....................................30

Useful addresses............................31

Index.......................................32

Animals as friends

Millions of people around the world keep pets.
Cats and dogs are great favourites. Other popular
pets include hamsters, goldfish, budgerigars,
guinea pigs and rabbits. Do you have a pet?

Wild dogs were the first animals that lived with people. They would hang around camp fires at night and wait for scraps of food.

Gradually these animals got used to living with people. They became domesticated, or tame.

The dogs we keep as pets today are related to the wolf family.

Now there are lots of different kinds of pets. Some people keep unusual animals, such as pot bellied pigs, stick insects or snakes.

People like to own animals because they keep them company and become friends.

Unusual pets need special care.

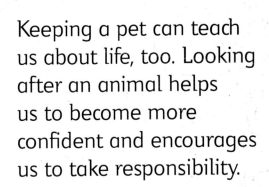

Keeping a pet can teach us about life, too. Looking after an animal helps us to become more confident and encourages us to take responsibility.

Taking care of our pets keeps us fit and healthy. Our pets can also help to protect us.

It's exciting to have a pet of your own.

Good company

Having a pet helps people to feel wanted – and not so alone. It can be comforting to see a dog with a wagging tail, hear a cat purring in front of the fire, or listen to the sound of a bird chirping from its cage. People who live alone find it reassuring to know that there is someone else in the house to keep them company.

Having a pet gives people somebody else to talk to – and it's usually someone who will always listen.

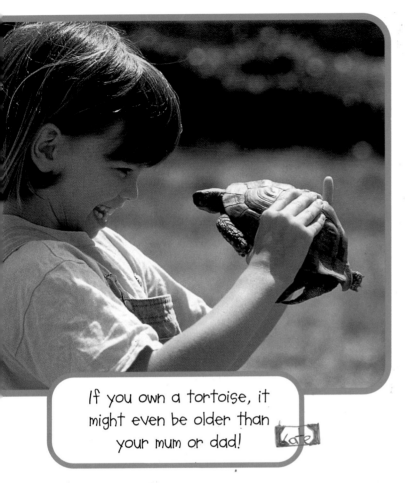

Many small pets, such as hamsters and gerbils, only live for a few years. A cat can live for as long as 20 years. Some animals, such as tortoises and snakes, have very long lives — they can live to be 40 years old or more.

Whether pets are with us for a short time or for many years, they are usually an important part of the family.

If you own a tortoise, it might even be older than your mum or dad!

Animal Anecdote

Wil Cwac Cwac is one of the oldest ducks on record.

When he reached his 25th birthday his owners celebrated by making a special birthday cake with 25 candles on it. It was one of his favourites — sponge cake filled with cream.

Planning ahead

Choosing a pet and taking it home is very exciting. It is the beginning of a new friendship. But looking after a pet is also a big responsibility.

Once a pet has been taken home, it needs to be looked after for the rest of its life.

It's important not to lose interest and forget about a new pet. Animals depend on their owners to bring them their food and water.

Pets that are picked up and played with a lot soon become friendly.

Many small pets, such as hamsters and guinea pigs, live in cages. Their bedding has to be changed and their food and water containers washed every day. Large pets need a lot of looking after, too.

Caring for a pet teaches us to take responsibility for others. It also helps us to practise organising and planning our time so we can fit in *all* the things we want to do.

Ponies have to be fed, watered, groomed and exercised. That's a lot to fit into one day.

Training your pet

One of the responsibilities of owning a pet is making sure that it is well trained. A well-behaved pet is much nicer to live with.

Training an animal can teach you a lot about yourself. You learn to be patient — it can take a long time for an animal to learn new things.

It's important to be consistent, always behaving in the same way. For example, you should always use the same word when you give a command, rather than a similar word which could confuse your pet.

Training your pet can be good fun.

Animal Anecdote

Sparkie the budgerigar was taught to say 531 words, 383 sentences and 8 nursery rhymes.

Because Sparkie was such a talkative bird he became quite famous. He was asked to appear on many television shows.

Sometimes you might feel like giving up, but you have to be firm and make sure your pet does everything properly. Most importantly, you have to find time each day for your training sessions. How well your pet behaves will show how well you have done your job.

House-training a pet is very important. The number of 'accidents' it has is one way to find out how well your training has worked!

A healthy life

Some pets need a lot of exercise if they are to stay fit and healthy. Dogs must be allowed to run around outside to use up all their energy. They love to fetch sticks, run after balls and go for walks.

Taking the dog for a walk every day not only keeps the dog fit, but can help to make the whole family fit and healthy too!

Going for a walk every day is good for you as well as your dog.

Horses and ponies need plenty of exercise. They should be let out into a field every day, or taken for a ride.

Riding also helps to keep people fit. The rider has to work hard — riding uses muscles in the arms, legs and back.

Big animals, such as horses, need exercising every day.

Give your pet plenty of toys, and also play with it yourself. The more time you spend with your pet, the better you get to know it. People find that playing with an animal is very relaxing, as well as fun.

Toys help to make your pets' lives more interesting.

Learning to relax

There are many things that can make people worry. Sometimes it's because we don't feel well, or because we have to take an exam, or start at a new school or job. Owning and caring for a pet can help us to relax and keep calm.

When people stroke or talk to their pets, they become much more relaxed. While they are thinking about their pet's needs, they forget their own worries.

It feels good to cuddle a purring cat.

Scientific tests show that looking after and stroking pets can improve people's health.

Often, elderly people in hospitals or nursing homes cannot keep pets. Some pet owners take their animals to visit so the patients still get the benefit of being able to stroke and talk to animals.

Taking care of a pet gives people something to think about.

The calming effect of animals helps people in other ways too.

Some people get nervous when they visit the doctor or dentist. Scientists found that putting an aquarium (fish tank) in waiting rooms helped patients to relax. They watched the fish swimming about and forgot to worry.

Feeling proud

Most pets need to be groomed regularly. Grooming helps to keep your pet healthy, and it makes it look good, too.

Grooming your pet is fun. You soon become an expert hairdresser!

Many people like to enter their pets for pet shows. There are often prizes for the best groomed pet, the strangest pet, or the dog with the 'waggiest' tail.

Winning a prize at a pet show is very exciting. It is a reward for all the hard work you have done to keep your pet healthy and well. Winning a prize can also make you feel proud.

There are many proud owners hoping to win a prize at this cat show.

Animal Anecdote

'On the day of my first pony show I spent all morning brushing my pony so he was all shiny. When we got to the show I was really nervous – I started to shake. I couldn't believe it when we won a prize. I was really happy – but I was still shaking!'

Anna, aged 8.

17

A sixth sense?

We have five senses – sight, smell, hearing, taste and touch. But many animals sense things that we cannot. Mice and cats feel the tiniest vibrations in the ground, and hear sounds too high for us to hear. Some animals are very good at seeing in the dark, when we can see very little, or can smell things that we don't notice.

Cats can see well in the dark.

Some pets seem to know when their owners are coming home. They wait by the door or look out of the window. Scientists don't know how animals can sense their owners' return. Perhaps they have an extra sixth sense?

Some pets are able to tell when their owners are going to return home from holiday!

Sometimes the way animals can sense things we don't notice can protect people. Some animals can feel changes that mean danger. By watching their pets, people living in an earthquake zone may get an early warning before danger strikes. Many animals start running to and fro, calling out and trying to get out of buildings.

If a pet behaves in an odd way it may be trying to warn us of danger.

Animal Anecdote

Thomas, the cat, lives with his owner, May, in Florida, in the United States. One day Thomas was restless and wouldn't eat. Early the next morning, he woke May by scratching her face. May decided that Thomas was trying to warn her about something and together they left the house. Just one hour later there was an earthquake and the house was destroyed.

Pets for protection

Animals are often used to protect us. Large dogs can be frightening. This is why certain breeds, such as German Shepherds, Dobermans and Rottweilers, are used as guard dogs. They patrol buildings and industrial estates.

The family dog can help to protect us and our homes. A dog barking will help to put off unwanted visitors.

A fierce-looking dog will stop even the bravest person in their tracks.

Some guard animals are more unusual. Geese can be quite fierce. Male geese, or ganders, can be very frightening when they run towards you with their heads down and wings out. This makes them good at guarding a house or farm. Their honking and hissing can be heard for some distance.

Geese hiss and even spit! They can look very frightening.

Animal Anecdote

Pigs have a very strong sense of smell. When pet pig Snort smelled gas leaking from a gas tap, she alerted her owners to the danger by oinking loudly and running around. Her owners called the fire brigade, who traced the leak. Snort was given an award for helping to stop an explosion which saved her owners' lives.

21

Saving lives

Pets and their owners can become very close. Sometimes the friendship between a pet and its owner is so strong that if something happens to the owner, the animal will try to help.

Dogs may go for help when their owners have had an accident. They bark at people to attract attention. Rescuers then follow the dogs to where their owners are lying hurt.

A barking dog can attract attention when there is a problem so help can be called.

There are stories, too, of horses who have gone for help when their riders have fallen off. The horses have returned to the stable yard and raised the alarm.

Horses sometimes help their injured riders.

Animal Anecdote

Fen, a border collie, was a friendly and lovable dog. His owner, Matt, enjoyed sailing. He often took Fen out on the boat with him. One day, Matt slipped and fell into the water. Fen was quick to leap into the water after him to pull Matt to safety.

The way home

The friendship between owner and pet can be very special. There are many stories of animals that have become separated from their owners and yet managed to track their owners down.

People and pets can be such good friends that they don't like to be apart.

Sometimes, when people go on holiday, they leave their pets to be cared for, in a kennel or cattery for example. Some animals manage to escape and find their way back home, even when it means travelling a very long way.

Pets may go into special homes while their owners are on holiday.

Homing pigeons are amazing birds. They become very attached to their homes and owners.

When they are freed, they do not fly off into the wild. Instead they return to the loft where they live and are cared for.

Homing pigeons can be released hundreds of kilometres from their home and still manage to find their way back.

Animal Anecdote

Sugar the cat was born in California. When she was two years old, her owner had to move 2,400 kms to Oklahoma. Sugar was left with a friend. Very soon Sugar went missing – it was thought she had died. Then, 14 months later, she turned up in the garden of her old owner's new house. Somehow she had followed her owner across the United States to a place she had never even visited.

Saying goodbye

There are times when people have to say goodbye to their pets: people may move from one country to another and may not be able to take their animals with them; children who have their own ponies will have to sell them when they grow too big to ride them.

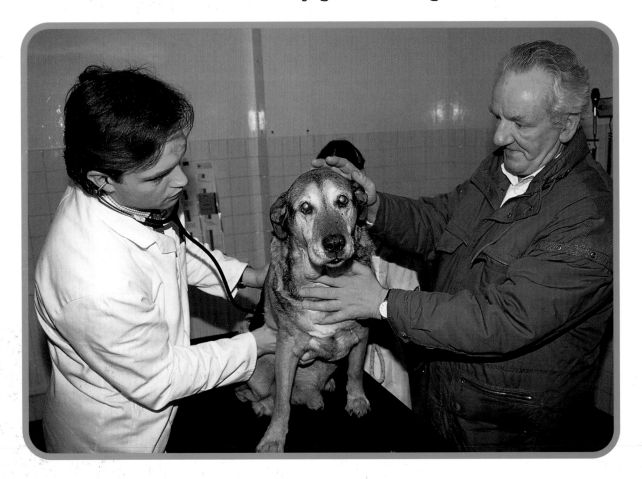

Sometimes pets become ill and die. It is very sad when a pet dies, especially if it has been part of the family for many years.

Saying goodbye to a pet can be one of the hardest things a person has to do, but it is part of the responsibilities of being a pet-owner.

Many older people worry about what will happen to their pet if they die. They may ask a friend to look after it.

The strong feelings that some people have for their pets is shown when they leave money in their will to make sure that their pets will always be cared for.

Animal Anecdote

One of the richest dogs in the world is called Gunther. He was left £40 million by his owner.

Gunther lives in Italy where he is very well looked after. He has a car and chauffeur to drive him around the countryside and take him for walks. He also owns a local football team!

27

Old friends

Many pets, whether they are large or small, become an important part of the family. The family grows up with its pets, getting older together.

The animals take on a very important role — always being there for comfort and company, seeing their owners through happy and sad times.

If you own a pet you are the most important person in that pet's life and probably its best friend. In return for being well looked after, pets give their owners endless love and affection. And sometimes, people may even owe them their lives.

Animal Anecdote

Philip has had Toby since he was a puppy — they have grown old together. One day, as Philip and Toby were on their daily walk, Philip stumbled and fell — and he didn't get up. Toby nuzzled Philip to wake him up. When Philip didn't move, Toby barked and barked. He attracted the attention of other people who came to the rescue.

Philip is proud of his dog, 'Toby and I have been friends for a long time. He saved my life.'

29

Glossary

affection	a feeling of liking or love.
comforting	when something makes us feel relaxed and happy.
companion	a friend.
confident	when you feel certain about what you are doing and believe in yourself.
consistent	not changing, doing the same thing.
to depend on	to look to someone else to do something for you.
domesticated	when something has become used to living with people; when it has been tamed.
grooming	the action of looking after something, making it look smart.
loft	the space under a roof in a building.
patrol	to walk around an area and keep guard.
proud	when you feel pleased with yourself.
responsibility	when you have to take care of something or carry out certain duties.

Useful addresses

United Kingdom

**Blue Cross Animal
Welfare Charity**
Shilton Road
Burford
Oxfordshire
OX18 4PF
www.bluecross.org.uk

**National Canine
Defence League**
17 Wakely Street
London
EC1V 7RQ
www.ncdl.org.uk

Pet Protectors' Club, PDSA
Whitechapel Way
Priorslee, Telford
Shropshire
TF2 9PQ
www.pdsa.co.uk

Pets as Therapy
17 Ambrook Road
Reading
RG2 8SL
www.petsastherapy.org

RSPCA
The Causeway
Horsham
West Sussex
RH12 1HG
www.rspca.org.uk

The Cats Protection League
17 Kings Road
Horsham
West Sussex
RH13 5PN
www.cats.org.uk

Australia

RSPCA Sydney
201 Brookwood Road
PO Box 34
Yagoona
NSW 2199
www.rspca.org.au

Index

affection 29

birds 6
budgerigars 4

cats 4, 6, 7, 14, 18, 19,
  24, 25
chauffeur 27
companion 28

dogs 4, 6, 12, 20, 22, 23
  being domesticated 4
  on patrol 20
ducks 7

earthquake 19
exercise 12, 13

fish 15

geese 21
gerbils 7
grooming 9, 16, 17
guinea pigs 4, 9

hamsters 4, 7, 9
horses 13, 23

pets
  as friends 5, 22, 24, 28
  calming effect of 14, 15
  care of 8, 9, 16
  giving comfort 6, 28
  giving confidence 5
  responsibility for 5, 8,
    9, 10, 26
pet shows 16, 17
pigeons 25
  pigeon loft 25
pigs 5, 21
ponies 9, 13

rabbits 4
rescue 22

sixth sense 18, 19
snakes 5, 7
stick insects 5

tortoises 7
training 10, 11

vibration 18